Picnic Cookbook

Enjoy the Warm Weather with Delicious Picnic Recipes

By
BookSumo Press

Published by
http://www.booksumo.com

LEGAL NOTES

Table of Contents

Spicy Fried Chicken Wings 101 78

Messy Oven Fried Picnic Chicken 79

Maria's Buttermilk Chicken 80

Chicken Tenders 101 w/ Spicy Dipping Sauce 81

The Perfect Gluten-Free Chicken Cutlet 82

Memphis Inspired Fried Chicken Breast 83

5 Star Fried Chicken 84

Curry Fried Chicken 85

Spiced Chicken 86

Easy Mexican Fried Chicken Chimichangas 87

American Potato Salad 88

Egg Salad 89

Chicken Salad 90

Corn Salad 91

Ensalada de Papas Colombiana (10-Ingredient Potato Salad) 92

Tuna Salad 93

Macaroni Salad 94

Mesa Macaroni Salad 95

Maque Choux (Native American Style Corn Salad) 96

Ceviche Guatemala Style 97

Chipotle Cannellini Burgers 98

Beast Burger 99

Parmesan Kernels Burger 100

Cheesy Italian Pizza Burger 101

BALSAMIC
Mayo Burgers

Prep Time: 15 mins
Total Time: 2 h 40 mins

Servings per Recipe: 4
Calories	375 kcal
Fat	22.5 g
Carbohydrates	337.8g
Protein	7.1 g
Cholesterol	21 mg
Sodium	2459 mg

Ingredients
4 large Portobello mushroom caps
1/2 C. soy sauce
1/2 C. balsamic vinegar
4 cloves garlic, chopped, or more to taste
1 large red bell pepper
1 C. reduced-fat mayonnaise
1 tbsp cayenne pepper, or to taste
4 hamburger buns split

Directions
1. Get a zip lock bag: Add the mushroom with soy sauce, balsamic vinegar, and garlic. Shake the bag roughly to coat the ingredients. Place it aside for 2 h 30 min.
2. Before you do anything heat the grill and grease it.
3. Cook the bell pepper for 6 min on each side. Drain the mushroom caps from the marinade and cook them for 7 min on each side.
4. Transfer the bell pepper to a zip lock bag and seal it and place them aside for 5 min sweat. Peel the bell peppers and chop them.
5. Get a mixing bowl: Add the roasted bell pepper with mayo and cayenne pepper. Mix them well. Place it in the fridge until ready to serve.
6. Assemble your burgers with your favorite toppings. Serve them right away.
7. Enjoy.

Onion
Bread

Prep Time: 3 hr 20 mins
Total Time: 3 hr 20 mins

Servings per Recipe: 8
Calories   260 kcal
Fat   5.3 g
Carbohydrates   45.9 g
Protein   6.9 g
Cholesterol   13 mg
Sodium   487 mg

Ingredients

3/4 C. lukewarm milk
5 tbsps lukewarm water
3 tbsps butter, softened
1 1/2 tsps salt
3 tbsps white sugar
1 tsp onion powder
3 tbsps dried minced onion

1/4 C. instant potato flakes
3 C. all-purpose flour
1 (.25 oz.) envelope active dry yeast
1 egg white
1 tbsp water
1/4 C. dried minced onion

Directions

1. Add the following to a bread machine and set the machine to the dough cycle: yeast, milk, flour, water, potato flakes, butter, 3 tbsps of dried onions, salt, onion powder, and sugar.
2. Now work the dough on a cutting board coated with flour for 2 mins then slice the dough into 8 pieces.
3. Shape each piece into a ball then flatten each one.
4. Place the flattened dough in a jellyroll pan which has been coated with nonstick spray and place a kitchen towel over everything.
5. Let the dough sit for 50 mins.
6. Now set your oven to 350 degrees before doing anything else.
7. Get a small bowl and whisk your water and egg together. Top the rolls with the egg wash then coat each one with the rest of the minced onions.
8. Cook everything in the oven for 17 mins.
9. Enjoy.

BREAD
Bolognese

Prep Time: 20 mins
Total Time: 3 hr 20 mins

Servings per Recipe: 20	
Calories	105 kcal
Fat	0.9 g
Carbohydrates	20.6g
Protein	3.1 g
Cholesterol	9 mg
Sodium	179 mg

Ingredients

4 C. unbleached all-purpose flour
1 tbsp light brown sugar
1 1/3 C. warm water (110 degrees F/45 degrees C)
1 1/2 tsp salt
1 1/2 tsp olive oil
1 (.25 oz.) package active dry yeast

1 egg
1 tbsp water
2 tbsp cornmeal

Directions

1. In the bread machine pan, place the flour, brown sugar, warm water, salt, olive oil and yeast in the order recommended by the manufacturer.
2. Select the Dough cycle and press Start.
3. Deflate the dough and transfer onto a lightly floured surface.
4. Shape the dough into two equal sized loaves.
5. Place the loaves, seam side down on a cutting board, sprinkled with the cornmeal generously.
6. With a damp cloth, cover the loaves and keep in warm place for about 40 minutes.
7. Set your oven to 375 degrees F.
8. In a small bowl, add the egg and 1 tbsp of the water and beat well.
9. Coat the loaves with the egg mixture and with a sharp knife, make a single long, quick cut down the center of the loaves.
10. Carefully, place the loaves onto a baking sheet
11. Cook in the oven for about 30-35 minutes.

Walnuts and Cinnamon Swirl

Servings per Recipe: 24
Calories	162 kcal
Fat	5.5 g
Carbohydrates	24.4g
Protein	4.1 g
Cholesterol	24 mg
Sodium	129 mg

Ingredients

1 C. milk
2 eggs
1/4 C. butter
4 C. bread flour
1/4 C. white sugar
1 tsp salt
1 1/2 tsp active dry yeast

1/2 C. chopped walnuts
1/2 C. packed brown sugar
2 tsp ground cinnamon
2 tbsp softened butter, divided
2 tsp sifted confectioners' sugar, divided (optional)

Directions

1. In the bread machine pan, place the milk, eggs, 1/4 C. of the butter, bread flour, sugar, salt, and yeast in the order recommended by the manufacturer.
2. Select the Dough setting and press Start.
3. After the dough cycle is completed, transfer the dough onto a floured surface and punch down.
4. Let the dough rest for about 10 minutes.
5. In a bowl, mix together walnuts, brown sugar and cinnamon.
6. Divide the dough in half and roll each half into a 9x14-inches rectangle.
7. Spread 1 tbsp of the softened butter over the top of each dough rectangle evenly and sprinkle with half of the walnut mixture.
8. Roll dough rectangles, starting from the short ends, and pinch seams closed.
9. Grease 2 (9x5-inch) loaf pans.
10. Place the rolled loaves into the prepared loaf pans, seam sides down.
11. Cover and keep in warm place for about 30 minutes.
12. Set your oven to 350 degrees F.
13. Cook in the oven for about 30 minutes.
14. Let the breads cool in the pans for about 10 minutes before removing to finish cooling on wire racks.
15. Sprinkle each loaf with 1 tsp of the confectioners' sugar.

CARDAMOM
Pearl Sugar
Coffee Bread

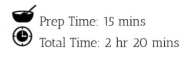

Prep Time: 15 mins

Total Time: 2 hr 20 mins

Servings per Recipe: 8

Calories	283 kcal
Fat	4.6 g
Carbohydrates	52.8g
Protein	7.5 g
Cholesterol	36 mg
Sodium	195 mg

Ingredients

1 C. milk
1/2 tsp salt
1 egg yolk
2 tbsp softened butter
3 C. all-purpose flour
1/3 C. sugar
1 (.25 oz.) envelope active dry yeast

3 tsp ground cardamom
2 egg whites, slightly beaten
pearl sugar

Directions

1. In the bread machine pan, place all the ingredients in the order recommended by the manufacturer.
2. Select the Dough cycle and press Start.
3. After the dough cycle is completed, divide into 3 equal portions.
4. Roll each portion into a 12-14-inches long rope.
5. Place the three ropes side by side, then braid together.
6. Tuck the ends underneath and place onto a greased baking sheet.
7. With a towel, cover loosely and keep in warm place to rise till doubled in size.
8. Set your oven to 375 degrees F.
9. Coat the loaf with the beaten egg and sprinkle with the pearl sugar.
10. Cook in the oven for about 20-25 minutes.

Buttermilk
Maple Bread

🍲 Prep Time: 1 hr 30 mins

🕐 Total Time: 3 d 11 hr

Servings per Recipe: 15

Calories	104 kcal
Fat	0.9 g
Carbohydrates	20.6 g
Protein	4.9 g
Cholesterol	13 mg
Sodium	124 mg

Ingredients
1/2 C. sprouted wheat berries, ground
3/4 C. buttermilk
1 egg
2 tbsp maple syrup
1/2 tsp salt
1/3 tsp baking soda
2 tbsp vital wheat gluten

2 1/4 C. whole wheat flour
1 1/2 tsp active dry yeast

Directions
1. Rinse 1/2 C. of the raw wheat berries in cool water and drain.
2. In a large bowl of the water, add the berries and soak, covered for 12 hours or overnight.
3. In a colander, drain the berries and keep, covered in a dark place.
4. Rinse for about 3 times a day and they will soon begin to sprout.
5. In a couple of days the sprouts will reach their optimum length of about 1/4-inch.
6. Drain the sprouts and in a food processor, grind them.
7. In the bread machine pan, place all the ingredients in the order recommended by the manufacturer.
8. Select the Whole Wheat cycle and Medium Crust setting and press Start.

BUTTERMILK
Brown Sugar Bread Rolls

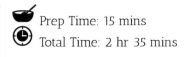

Prep Time: 15 mins

Total Time: 2 hr 35 mins

Servings per Recipe: 12

Calories	176 kcal
Fat	4.4 g
Carbohydrates	28.3g
Protein	5.2 g
Cholesterol	20 mg
Sodium	271 mg

Ingredients
3 C. bread flour
1 C. buttermilk
2 tbsp packed brown sugar
1 1/2 tsp kosher salt
1 (.25 oz.) package active dry yeast

1 egg yolk
2 tbsp canola oil
stick butter

Directions
1. In the bread machine pan, place the bread flour, buttermilk, brown sugar, salt, yeast and egg yolk.
2. Select the Dough setting and let the machine to mix the ingredients till moist.
3. Pause the cycle and add the oil, then let the machine continue to the end of the Dough cycle.
4. Grease the cups of the muffin pans and keep aside.
5. Punch down the dough and remove it from the machine.
6. Divide the dough into 12 equal portions and shape into round, smooth rolls.
7. Arrange the rolls into the prepared muffin cups.
8. Cover the rolls with a kitchen towel and keep in the warm place for about 25 minutes.
9. Set your oven to 350 degrees F.
10. Cook in the oven for about 20 minutes.
11. Remove from the oven and immediately, rub the tops of the hot rolls with a stick of the butter for a soft crust.
12. Cool the rolls slightly and serve warm.

Vegan
Cornmeal Muffins

Prep Time: 5 mins
Total Time: 20 min

Servings per Recipe: 6
Calories	177 kcal
Fat	5.4 g
Carbohydrates	31g
Protein	2.5 g
Cholesterol	0 mg
Sodium	310 mg

Ingredients
1/2 C. cornmeal
1/2 C. whole-wheat pastry flour
1/2 tsp baking soda
1/2 tsp salt

1/2 C. applesauce
1/2 C. soy milk
1/4 C. agave nectar
2 tbsp canola oil

Directions
1. Set your oven to 325 degrees F before doing anything else and lightly, grease 6 cups of a muffin pan.
2. In a large bowl, mix together the cornmeal, flour, baking soda and salt.
3. Add the applesauce, soy milk and agave nectar and stir to combine.
4. Slowly add the oil. Stirring continuously till well combined.
5. Transfer the mixture into the prepared muffin cups evenly.
6. Cook in the oven for about 15-20 minutes or till a toothpick inserted in the center comes out clean

CINNAMON
Pecan Muffins

Prep Time: 15 mins
Total Time: 35 mins

Servings per Recipe: 12
Calories	227 kcal
Fat	13 g
Carbohydrates	25.6g
Protein	2.9 g
Cholesterol	16 mg
Sodium	212 mg

Ingredients

1 1/2 C. all-purpose flour
1/2 C. white sugar
1/4 C. brown sugar
1 tsp baking soda
1 tsp ground cinnamon
1/2 tsp salt
1/2 C. olive oil

1/4 C. milk
1 egg
1 1/2 tsp vanilla extract
1 C. shredded zucchini
1/2 C. fresh blueberries
1/2 C. chopped pecans

Directions

1. Set your oven to 350 degrees F before doing anything else and grease 12 cups of a muffin pan.
2. In a bowl, mix together the flour, white sugar, brown sugar, baking soda, cinnamon and salt.
3. In another bowl, add the olive oil, milk, egg and vanilla extract and beat till smooth.
4. Add the egg mixture into the flour mixture and mix till just moistened.
5. Fold in the zucchini, blueberries and pecans.
6. Transfer the mixture into the prepared muffin cups about 2/3 full.
7. Cook in the oven for about 20-25 minutes or till a toothpick inserted in the center comes out clean.

Lunch Box
Muffins

🥣 Prep Time: 15 mins
🕐 Total Time: 1 hr

Servings per Recipe: 12
Calories	240 kcal
Fat	13.4 g
Carbohydrates	28.2g
Protein	3.4 g
Cholesterol	16 mg
Sodium	171 mg

Ingredients

1 C. whole wheat flour
1/2 C. all-purpose flour
3/4 C. white sugar
1 1/2 tsp baking powder
1/2 tsp salt
1/2 C. low-fat vanilla yogurt
1/2 C. canola oil

1 egg
2 tsp vanilla extract
1 ripe pear - peeled, cored, and diced
1/2 C. chopped pecans

Directions

1. Set your oven to 450 degrees F before doing anything else and line 12 cups of a muffin pan with the paper liners.
2. In a bowl, mix together the flours, sugar, baking powder and salt.
3. In another bowl, add the yogurt, oil, egg and vanilla extract and beat till smooth.
4. Add the yogurt mixture into the flour mixture and mix till just combined.
5. Fold in the pear and pecans.
6. Transfer the mixture into the prepared muffin cups evenly.
7. Place the muffin pan in the oven and immediately, set it to 350 degrees F.
8. Cook in the oven for about 20-25 minutes or till a toothpick inserted in the center comes out clean.
9. Remove from the oven and cool for about 5 minutes before turning out onto wire rack to cool completely.

HONEY
Almond Muffins

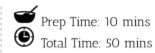

Prep Time: 10 mins
Total Time: 50 mins

Servings per Recipe: 12
Calories	107 kcal
Fat	6.6 g
Carbohydrates	10.3g
Protein	2.3 g
Cholesterol	31 mg
Sodium	40 mg

Ingredients
2 eggs, separated
2 tbsp margarine, softened
2 tbsp honey
1/4 tsp almond extract
1/3 C. boiling water

3/4 C. unsweetened flaked coconut
3/4 C. all-purpose flour

Directions
1. Set your oven to 350 degrees F before doing anything else and grease 12 cups of a muffin pan.
2. In a large bowl add the egg yolks and beat.
3. Add the butter, honey, almond extract, boiling water, coconut and flour and mix till just combined.
4. In another bowl, add the egg whites and with an electric mixer, beat till stiff.
5. Fold the egg whites into the flour mixture.
6. Transfer the mixture into the prepared muffin cups about 2/3 full.
7. Cook in the oven for about 20-25 minutes or till a toothpick inserted in the center comes out clean.

Caribbean
Rolled Oats Muffins

Prep Time: 15 mins
Total Time: 45 mins

Servings per Recipe: 12
Calories	158 kcal
Fat	4.9 g
Carbohydrates	26.6g
Protein	3.3 g
Cholesterol	16 mg
Sodium	129 mg

Ingredients

1 C. water
1/2 C. rolled oats
1 1/2 C. all-purpose flour
1/4 C. wheat bran
1/3 C. white sugar
4 tsp baking powder
1/8 tsp ground nutmeg

1 mashed banana
1 beaten egg
1 (8 oz.) can crushed pineapple, well drained
1 C. coconut milk
1/8 tsp coconut extract

Directions

1. In a pan, add the water and bring to a boil.
2. Stir in the oats and cook for about 1 minute.
3. Cover and remove from the heat, then keep aside to cool.
4. Set your oven to 375 degrees F before doing anything else and grease and flour 12 cups of a muffin pan.
5. In a large bowl, mix together the flour, bran, sugar, baking powder and nutmeg.
6. Make a well in the center of the mixture.
7. In the well, add the mashed banana, cooled oatmeal, egg, pineapple, coconut milk and coconut extract and mix till smooth.
8. Transfer the mixture into the prepared muffin cups evenly.
9. Cook in the oven for about 25-30 minutes or till a toothpick inserted in the center comes out clean.

HOMEMADE
Ciabatta Rolls

🥣 Prep Time: 30 mins
🕐 Total Time: 2 hr

Servings per Recipe: 24
Calories	73 kcal
Fat	0.9 g
Carbohydrates	13.7g
Protein	2.3 g
Cholesterol	0 mg
Sodium	146 mg

Ingredients
1 1/2 C. water
1 1/2 tsp salt
1 tsp white sugar
1 tbsp olive oil

3 1/4 C. bread flour
1 1/2 tsp bread machine yeast

Directions
1. In the bread machine pan, place all the ingredients in the order recommended by the manufacturer.
2. Select the Dough cycle and press Start.
3. After the cycle is completed, transfer the dough onto a generously floured surface.
4. With a greased plastic wrap, cover the dough and keep aside for about 15 minutes.
5. Line the baking sheets with the parchment papers.
6. Divide the dough into 2 portions and shape each into a 3x14-inch oval.
7. Arrange the loaves onto prepared sheets and dust lightly with the flour.
8. Cover and place in warm place for about 45 minutes.
9. Set your oven to 425 degrees F.
10. Drizzle the loaves with the water.
11. Arrange the loaves in the middle rack of the oven and cook for about 25-30 minutes.

Feta
Bread

Prep Time: 15 mins

Total Time: 1 h 15 mins

Servings per Recipe: 10	
Calories	258 kcal
Fat	8.2 g
Carbohydrates	37.5g
Protein	8 g
Cholesterol	16 mg
Sodium	502 mg

Ingredients

1 1/4 C. water
2 tbsp butter
2 tbsp white sugar
2 tbsp milk powder
1 1/2 tsp salt
3 1/3 C. bread flour
1 1/2 tsp active dry yeast

2 tbsp olive oil
2 tsp garlic powder (optional)
4 oz. crumbled feta cheese (optional)

Directions

1. In the bread machine pan, place the water, butter, white sugar, milk powder, salt, bread flour and active dry yeast in the order recommended by the manufacturer.
2. Select the Dough cycle and press Start.
3. Set your outdoor grill for medium heat.
4. After the cycle is completed, transfer the dough onto a lightly floured surface and divide into 2 halves.
5. Roll each half into a 9-10-inches circle.
6. Coat the top of each circle with the olive oil.
7. Place the bread circles oil side down onto the grill and coat the other side with the olive oil.
8. Cook on the grill till the bottom side is browned.
9. Flip the side and cook on the grill till golden.
10. Serve with a sprinkling of the garlic powder and feta cheese.

SOUTHERN
Spicy Cornbread

🥣 Prep Time: 3 hr
🕐 Total Time: 3 hr 35 min

Servings per Recipe: 12
Calories	190 kcal
Fat	3.4 g
Carbohydrates	33.5g
Protein	6.3 g
Cholesterol	16 mg
Sodium	215 mg

Ingredients
1 1/4 C. water
1 egg
1/4 C. nonfat dry milk powder
1 tsp salt
2 tbsp white sugar
2 tbsp shortening
3 C. bread flour or all-purpose flour
1/3 C. cornmeal

2/3 C. frozen corn kernels, thawed and drained
1 1/2 tsp red pepper flakes
1 tsp bread machine yeast

Directions
1. In the bread machine pan, place all the ingredients in the order recommended by the manufacturer.
2. Set the pan in the machine and close the lid.
3. Select the Dough cycle and press start.
4. When the cycle is completed, transfer the dough onto a lightly floured surface and press out all of the air.
5. Roll the dough into a tight loaf and pinch the seam.
6. In a 9x5-inch loaf pan, place the loaf and keep aside for about 40 minutes.
7. Set your oven to 375 degrees F.
8. Cook in the oven for about 30-35 minutes.

Sourdough
Bread II

🥣 Prep Time: 10 mins
🕐 Total Time: 1 h 30 mins

Servings per Recipe: 12
Calories   167 kcal
Fat   1.6 g
Carbohydrates   32.4g
Protein   5.2 g
Cholesterol   1 mg
Sodium   201 mg

Ingredients

1 1/4 C. sourdough starter
1/3 C. water
3 C. all-purpose flour
1 tbsp white sugar
1 tbsp vegetable oil

1 tsp salt
2 tsp bread machine yeast

Directions

1. Allow the starter to come to room temperature.
2. In the bread machine pan, place all the ingredients in the order recommended by the manufacturer.
3. Select the Basic or White Bread cycle and Medium crust setting.
4. Press Start.

RAISIN
Bread

Prep Time: 5 mins
Total Time: 3 hr 5 min

Servings per Recipe: 15

Calories	175 kcal
Fat	3.5 g
Carbohydrates	31.7g
Protein	4.7 g
Cholesterol	20 mg
Sodium	185 mg

Ingredients

1 C. milk, room temperature
3 tbsp butter, softened
3 tbsp honey
1 tbsp brown sugar
1 egg, room temperature
1 tsp salt

1 tsp ground cinnamon
3 C. bread flour
2 1/4 tsp bread machine yeast
1 C. raisins

Directions

1. In the bread machine pan, place all the ingredients except the raisins in the order recommended by the manufacturer.
2. Set the bread maker on Sweet Dough setting.
3. Add the raisins at the signal or about 5 minutes before the kneading cycle has finished.

Roast Beef and Provolone Sandwich

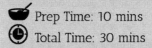 Prep Time: 10 mins

Total Time: 30 mins

Servings per Recipe: 4

Calories	548 kcal
Fat	22.6 g
Carbohydrates	40.5g
Protein	44.6 g
Cholesterol	94 mg
Sodium	2310 mg

Ingredients

1 (10.5 oz.) can beef consommé
1 C. water
1 lb thinly sliced deli roast beef

8 slices provolone cheese
4 hoagie rolls, split lengthwise

Directions

1. Set your oven to 350 degrees before doing anything else.
2. Open your rolls and place them in a casserole dish.
3. Now combine water and beef consommé in a pan to make a broth.
4. Cook your beef in this mixture for 5 mins.
5. Then divide the meat between your rolls and top them with cheese.
6. Cook the rolls in the oven for 6 mins.
7. Enjoy the sandwiches dipped in broth.

OREGANO
Mozzarella Sandwich

Prep Time: 10 mins
Total Time: 15 min

Servings per Recipe: 6
Calories	394 kcal
Fat	18.3 g
Carbohydrates	42g
Protein	15 g
Cholesterol	46 mg
Sodium	1032 mg

Ingredients
1/4 C. unsalted butter
1/8 tsp garlic powder (optional)
12 slices white bread
1 tsp dried oregano

1 (8 oz.) package shredded mozzarella cheese
1 (24 oz.) jar vodka marinara sauce

Directions
1. Turn on the broiler before doing anything else
2. Get a baking dish and lay half of your bread pieces in it.
3. On top of each piece of bread put some mozzarella. Then top the cheese with the remaining pieces of bread.
4. With a butter knife coat each sandwich with some butter. Then season the butter by applying some oregano and garlic powder.
5. Broil the sandwiches for 4 mins then flip it and apply more butter, oregano, and garlic to its opposite side.
6. Continue broiling the sandwich for another 4 mins.
7. Enjoy with the marinara as a dip.

Banh Mi
Sandwich

Prep Time: 10 mins
Total Time: 15 mins

Servings per Recipe: 4
Calories	627 kcal
Carbohydrates	72.1 g
Cholesterol	124 mg
Fat	12.1 g
Fiber	3.3 g
Protein	55.3 g
Sodium	1005 mg

Ingredients

4 boneless chicken breast, cut 1/4 inch thick
4 (7 inch) French bread baguettes, split lengthwise
4 tsps mayonnaise, or to taste
1 oz. chili sauce with garlic
1/4 C. fresh lime juice

1 small red onion, sliced into rings
1 medium cucumber, peeled and sliced lengthwise
2 tbsps chopped fresh cilantro
salt and pepper to taste

Directions

1. Place your chicken breast on a broiling pan and cook everything in the oven for 7 minutes, each side, or until the meat is fully done.
2. Put mayonnaise evenly on the French rolls and also put one pork chop on each roll.
3. Layer some chili sauce over the meat and add some lime juice, while topping it with onion, pepper, cucumber, salt and cilantro.
4. Add some more lime juice just before serving.

TOASTED
Cinnamon
Sandwich

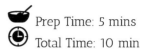 Prep Time: 5 mins
Total Time: 10 min

Servings per Recipe: 1
Calories   469 kcal
Fat   26.6 g
Carbohydrates   37.3g
Protein   20 g
Cholesterol   80 mg
Sodium   907 mg

Ingredients
2 links beef sausage links
1 slice Cheddar cheese
2 frozen waffles, toasted
1/4 Red Delicious apple, sliced very thin
1/2 tsp cinnamon-sugar

Directions
1. Stir fry your sausage for 6 mins until it is fully done.
2. Lay one piece of cheese on a waffle then place your apples on top of the cheese.
3. Top the apples with the cinnamon-sugar and the sausage.
4. Place the apples over the waffles and slice the sandwich in half.
5. Enjoy.

The Best
Egg Salad Sandwich

🥣 Prep Time: 10 mins
🕐 Total Time: 35 mins

Servings per Recipe: 4	
Calories	344 kcal
Fat	31.9 g
Carbohydrates	2.3g
Protein	< 13 g
Cholesterol	382 mg
Sodium	1351 mg

Ingredients

8 eggs
1/2 C. mayonnaise
1 tsp prepared yellow mustard
1/4 C. chopped green onion

salt and pepper to taste
1/4 tsp paprika

Directions

1. Get your eggs boiling in water.
2. Once the water is boiling, shut the heat, place a lid on the pot, and let the eggs sit in the water for 15 mins.
3. Drain the liquid, remove the shells, and dice the eggs.
4. Now grab a bowl, combine: green onions, eggs, mustard, and mayo.
5. Stir the mix until it is smooth and even then top everything with the paprika, some pepper, and salt.
6. Stir the mix again then serve the salad on some warmed bread rolls.
7. Enjoy.

PESTO
Provolone American Sandwich

Prep Time: 5 mins
Total Time: 15 mins

Servings per Recipe: 1
Calories   503 kcal
Fat   36.5 g
Carbohydrates   24.2g
Protein   20.4 g
Cholesterol   82 mg
Sodium   1108 mg

Ingredients
2 slices Italian bread
1 tbsp softened butter, divided
1 tbsp prepared pesto sauce, divided
1 slice provolone cheese
2 slices tomato
1 slice American cheese

Directions
1. Coat a piece of bread with butter and place the bread in a frying pan with the buttered side facing downwards.
2. Top the bread with 1/2 of the pesto sauce, some tomato, 1 piece of provolone, and 1 piece of American.
3. Grab the other piece of bread and coat it with the rest of the pesto and place the pesto side of the bread on top of the cheese.
4. Coat the top of the bread with more butter and cook the sandwich for 6 mins each side.
5. Enjoy.

Vodka
Sauce Sandwich

🥣 Prep Time: 10 mins
🕐 Total Time: 30 mins

Servings per Recipe: 6
Calories   394 kcal
Fat   18.3 g
Carbohydrates   42g
Protein   15 g
Cholesterol   46 mg
Sodium   1032 mg

Ingredients
1/4 C. unsalted butter
1/8 tsp garlic powder
12 slices white bread
1 tsp dried oregano

1 (8 oz.) package shredded mozzarella cheese
1 (24 oz.) jar vodka marinara sauce

Directions
1. Get your oven's broiler hot before doing anything else.
2. Grab a jelly roll pan and layer 6 pieces of bread in it.
3. Top the bread evenly with some mozzarella then place the remaining bread pieces.
4. Get a bowl, combine: garlic powder and butter.
5. Top the sandwiches with 1 tbsp of the butter mix. Then coat everything with some oregano.
6. Broil the sandwiches for 3 mins then turn the sandwiches over and coat the bread with another tbsp of butter and more oregano.
7. Continue broiling for 3 more mins then divide the sandwiches into 2 pieces.
8. Enjoy dipped in the marinara sauce.

WACO TEXAS
Tabasco Steak Sandwiches

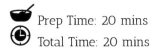 Prep Time: 20 mins

Total Time: 20 mins

Servings per Recipe: 4
Calories	337.1
Fat	24.6g
Cholesterol	61.0mg
Sodium	567.5mg
Carbohydrates	25.9g
Protein	3.9g

Ingredients
2 lb. cube steaks, sliced
1 large onion, sliced
4 deli French rolls
1/2 C. butter
1/2 tsp seasoning salt

1/2 C. Worcestershire sauce
5 dashes Tabasco sauce

Directions
1. In a skillet, add 2 tbsp of the butter over medium heat and cook until melted.
2. Add the onion and cook for about 7-8 minutes, stirring occasionally.
3. With a slotted spoon, transfer the onion into a bowl and keep aside.
4. Meanwhile, season the steak slices with the seasoned salt.
5. In the same skillet, add 2 tbsp of the butter over high heat and cook until melted.
6. Place the steak slices in a single layer and cook for about 1 minute per side.
7. Add the cooked onions, 2 tbsp of the butter, Worcestershire sauce and Tabasco sauce and mix well.
8. Place the remaining butter over French roll halves evenly.
9. Heat a skillet and cook the French roll halves until golden.
10. Arrange the bottom half of French rolls onto serving plates.
11. Place 1/4 of the meat mixture with some pan juices over each bottom half.
12. Cover with top half of the roll.
13. Cut each roll in half and enjoy.

Mexican
Pepper Sandwiches

🥣 Prep Time: 15 mins
🕐 Total Time: 15 mins

Servings per Recipe: 3
Calories	420.2
Fat	24.0g
Cholesterol	180.6mg
Sodium	563.0mg
Carbohydrates	33.1g
Protein	18.3g

Ingredients

1 (4 oz.) cans chopped green chilies, drained
6 slices bread
3 slices Monterey Jack cheese

2 eggs
1 C. milk
2 - 4 tbsp butter

Directions

1. In a bowl, add the chilies and with a fork, mash them.
2. Place the mashed chilies over 3 bread slices evenly, followed by the cheese.
3. Cover with the remaining bread slices.
4. In a bowl, add the milk and eggs and beat well.
5. Coat each sandwich with the egg mixture evenly.
6. In a skillet, add 2 tbsp of the butter and cook until melted.
7. Add the sandwiches and cook until golden brown from both sides.
8. Enjoy hot.

GROUND BEEF
Sandwiches

Prep Time: 10 mins
Total Time: 25 mins

Servings per Recipe: 6
Calories	264.6
Fat	9.7g
Cholesterol	49.1mg
Sodium	636.7mg
Carbohydrates	21.9g
Protein	20.4g

Ingredients

2 tbsp dried chopped onions
3 tbsp water
1 lb. lean ground beef
1 1/2 C. chicken broth
1/2 tsp salt
1/2 tsp pepper

6 hamburger buns
mustard
chopped onion

Directions

1. In a bowl, add the water and dried onions and keep aside until onions become just soft.
2. Heat a skillet over medium-high heat and cook the crumbled ground beef into a hot skillet and cook for about 2-3 minutes.
3. Add the soaked onions with any remaining water and cook until beef is no more pink, mixing frequently.
4. Add the salt, chicken broth and pepper and
5. cook for about 10 minutes.
6. Place the beef mixture onto buns, followed by the mustard and chopped onions and enjoy.

Vegetarian
Tomato Sandwich

🥣 Prep Time: 5 mins
🕐 Total Time: 5 mins

Servings per Recipe: 1
Calories	266.0
Fat	10.8g
Cholesterol	12.4mg
Sodium	655.7mg
Carbohydrates	37.0g
Protein	5.1g

Ingredients
2 slices bread toasted
1 medium organic tomato, sliced
3 tbsp Miracle Whip
salt

Directions
1. Place the Miracle Whip over both bread slices evenly.
2. Place the tomato slices onto one bread slice and sprinkle with the salt.
3. Cover with remaining bread slice and enjoy.

ARIZONA
Beef for Sandwiches

Prep Time: 5 mins
Total Time: 7 hr 5 mins

Servings per Recipe: 6
Calories	364.3
Fat	14.8g
Cholesterol	149.6mg
Sodium	1007.1mg
Carbohydrates	8.8g
Protein	49.4g

Ingredients
3 lb. chuck roast, trimmed
1 tsp salt
1 tsp pepper
2 tsp chili powder
2 tsp cumin
3 chipotle chilies in adobo, chopped
1 (4 oz.) cans green chilies

1 (7 oz.) cans salsa verde
1 C. sliced onion
3 tsp minced garlic
1 C. beef broth

Directions
1. In a crock pot chuck, add the chuck roast and sprinkle with the spices evenly.
2. Place the remaining ingredients on top evenly.
3. Set the crock pot on High and cook, covered for about 5 hours.
4. Uncover the crock pot and with 2 forks, shred the meat.
5. Set the crock pot on High and cook, covered for about 10-15 minutes.
6. Enjoy the meat in your desired sandwich alongside the pan juices as dipping sauce.

Reuben
Sandwich

🥣 Prep Time: 10 mins
🕐 Total Time: 20 mins

Servings per Recipe: 1	
Calories	760 kcal
Fat	43.9 g
Carbohydrates	48.9g
Protein	44.7 g
Cholesterol	150 mg
Sodium	3088 mg

Ingredients

1 C. sauerkraut, drained
10 oz. sliced deli turkey meat
2 tbsps butter
4 slices marble rye bread
4 slices Swiss cheese

4 tbsps thousand island salad dressing, or to taste

Directions

1. Place the following in a bowl: turkey, and sauerkraut.
2. Place the mix in the microwave for 1 mins.
3. Now coat one side of each piece of bread with butter liberally then coat the other piece with some dressing.
4. Evenly distribute your Swiss, sauerkraut, and turkey on two pieces of bread.
5. Top the meat with the other piece of bread with its buttered side facing upwards.
6. Now fry your sandwiches with the buttered side facing downwards for 8 mins, flipping the sandwich halfway.
7. Enjoy.

CRANBERRY
Curry Sandwich

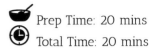

Prep Time: 20 mins
Total Time: 20 mins

Servings per Recipe: 6
Calories   528 kcal
Fat   32.7 g
Carbohydrates   43.9 g
Protein   16.5 g
Cholesterol   47 mg
Sodium   540 mg

Ingredients

2 C. cubed, cooked chicken
1 unpeeled red apple, chopped
3/4 C. dried cranberries
1/2 C. thinly sliced celery
1/4 C. chopped pecans
2 tbsps thinly sliced green onions
3/4 C. mayonnaise

2 tsps lime juice
1/2 tsp curry powder
12 slices bread
12 lettuce leaves

Directions

1. Get a bowl, combine: green onions, chicken, pecans, apple, celery, and cranberries.
2. Stir the mix then add in the curry, lime juice, and mayo.
3. Stir the mix again to working in the spices.
4. Place a covering of plastic on the bowl and put everything in the fridge until chilled.
5. Slice the crust off of the pieces of bread and liberally divide the chicken mix between half of the slices then top the mix with 1 piece of lettuce and layer the remaining pieces of bread to form a sandwich.
6. Enjoy.

Weekday
Simple Shrimp Sandwiches

Prep Time: 15 mins
Total Time: 15 mins

Servings per Recipe: 1
Calories	10.5
Fat	0.9g
Cholesterol	3.1mg
Sodium	17.2mg
Carbohydrates	0.3g
Protein	0.2g

Ingredients
1 (3 oz.) packages cream cheese
2 tbsp mayonnaise
1 tbsp catsup
1 tsp mustard
1 dash garlic powder

1 C. chopped canned shrimp
1/4 C. chopped celery
1 tsp chopped onion

Directions
1. In a blender, add all the ingredients and pulse until smooth.
2. Enjoy the shrimp mixture onto the buttered bread and enjoy.

CAROLINA
Dijon Coleslaw Sandwiches

 Prep Time: 10 mins
Total Time: 10 mins

Servings per Recipe: 2
Calories   380.9
Fat   28.1g
Cholesterol   99.6mg
Sodium   1119.7mg
Carbohydrates   9.9g
Protein   21.5g

Ingredients
1 C. Coleslaw, drained
2 tbsp dill, chopped
2 hard poppy seed rolls, split
1 tbsp Dijon mustard

4 slices salami
4 slices havarti cheese

Directions
1. In a bowl, add the coleslaw and dill and mix well.
2. Place the mustard onto top halves of each roll evenly.
3. Place the coleslaw mixture onto the bottom halves of each roll evenly, followed by the salami and cheese.
4. Cover each bottom half with the 1 top half. of the rolls.
5. Cut each sandwich in half and enjoy.

Provolone
Tuscan Sandwiches

Prep Time: 10 mins
Total Time: 15 mins

Servings per Recipe: 4
Calories	379.6
Fat	19.2g
Cholesterol	29.3mg
Sodium	657.9mg
Carbohydrates	34.4g
Protein	17.9g

Ingredients
1 (12 inch) baguette
2 tbsp olive oil
1/4 tsp dried oregano
1/4 tsp garlic powder

6 oz. provolone cheese, sliced
2 beefsteak tomatoes, sliced
salt and pepper

Directions
1. Set your grill for medium heat and lightly, grease the grill grate.
2. With a serrated knife, remove about 1/2-inch of the domed top of the baguette.
3. Now, cut the baguette in half horizontally.
4. In a bowl, add the oregano, garlic powder and oil and mix well.
5. Coat the both baguette halves with the oil mixture evenly.
6. Place 1/2 of the provolone cheese slices onto the bottom half of the baguette, followed by the tomato slices, salt, pepper and remaining provolone cheese slices.
7. Cover with the top half of the baguette.
8. Cook the sandwiches onto the grill for about 3 minutes.
9. Cut the sandwich into 4 equal sized portions and enjoy.

FLATBREAD
Turkey Club

Prep Time: 5 mins
Total Time: 10 mins

Servings per Recipe: 1
Calories	405.0
Fat	15.9 g
Cholesterol	77.9mg
Sodium	1449.5mg
Carbohydrates	40.0g
Protein	24.8g

Ingredients
2 slices Texas toast thick bread
3 oz. deli turkey, sliced thin
1 slice bacon, cooked crisp
2 slices tomatoes
mayonnaise

1 slice Swiss cheese
drizzle olive oil

Directions
1. Spread the mayonnaise over both bread slices evenly.
2. Place the turkey onto 1 bread slice, followed by the bacon, tomatoes and Swiss cheese.
3. Cover with the remaining bread slice.
4. Coat the sandwich with the oil from both sides.
5. Heat a grill pan and cook the sandwich until crisp from both sides.
6. Enjoy hot.

Mediterranean Chicken Pitas

Prep Time: 15 mins
Total Time: 15 mins

Servings per Recipe: 4
Calories   341.0
Fat   9.5g
Cholesterol   54.9mg
Sodium   772.1mg
Carbohydrates   37.0g
Protein   25.4g

Ingredients

1 (12 1/2 oz.) cans chunk chicken, drained
10 sprigs cilantro, chopped
1/2 medium lime, juice
1/4 medium cucumber, chopped
1 medium tomatoes, seeded and chopped
2 garlic cloves, minced
1/4 tsp dried oregano

1/4 tsp ground black pepper
1/2 tbsp extra virgin olive oil
4 -8 pita pockets

Directions

1. In a bowl, add all the ingredients and mix until well combined.
2. Place in the fridge for about 1 1/2 hours.
3. Place the mixture into 2 pita pocket halves evenly and enjoy.

CELIA'S
Chicken Caesar Sandwiches

Prep Time: 15 mins
Total Time: 45 mins

Servings per Recipe: 4
Calories   280.0
Fat   17.5g
Cholesterol   64.1mg
Sodium   619.5mg
Carbohydrates   9.2g
Protein   21.3g

Ingredients

2 roasted boneless skinless chicken breasts, sliced
4 oz. sliced pancetta
1 large garlic clove, chopped
2 tbsp chopped flat-leaf parsley
1 tsp Dijon mustard
1 1/2 tbsp lemon juice

1/2 C. mayonnaise
1 loaf ciabatta, halved horizontally
2 oz. romaine lettuce, chopped
3 oz. Parmesan cheese, grated

Directions

1. Set your oven to 350 degrees F before doing anything else.
2. In the bottom of a baking sheet, arrange the pancetta in a single layer.
3. Cook in the oven for about 10-15 minutes.
4. For the Caesar dressing: in a blender, add the parsley and garlic and pulse until minced.
5. Add the mayonnaise, mustard and lemon juice and pulse until smooth.
6. In a baking sheet, arrange the bread halves, cut side up and cook in the oven for about 5-7 minutes.
7. Remove from the oven and keep aside to cool slightly.
8. Place the Caesar dressing over cut side of each bread piece evenly.
9. Place half of the romaine onto the bottom half of the bread, followed by the Parmesan, pancetta and chicken.
10. Season with the salt and pepper evenly and top with the remaining romaine.
11. Cover with the top half of ciabatta.
12. Cut into 4 equal sized portions crosswise and enjoy.

Seattle
Backyard Sandwich

Prep Time: 10 mins
Total Time: 10 mins

Servings per Recipe: 4
Calories   591.7
Fat   18.1g
Cholesterol   19.3mg
Sodium   1089.7mg
Carbohydrates   85.0g
Protein   25.9g

Ingredients
8 slices sourdough bread
1/3 C. low-fat mayonnaise
1/4 C. Dijon mustard
4 romaine lettuce leaves
4 slices provolone cheese
1 large tomatoes, sliced
1 red onion, sliced

1 cucumber, peeled and halved lengthwise
1 - 2 avocado, peeled and sliced
1 (4 oz.) packages bean sprouts

Directions
1. Place the mayonnaise and Dijon mustard on one side of all bread slices.
2. Place 1 lettuce leaf on each of 4 bread slices, followed by 1 cheese slice, 1 tomato slice, onion slices, cucumber slices, and avocado slices and sprouts.
3. Cover each with the remaining bread slices.
4. Cut each sandwich in half diagonally and enjoy.

HOT DOGS
Seattle Style

Prep Time: 5 mins
Total Time: 25 mins

Servings per Recipe: 2
Calories	477.2
Fat	33.9g
Cholesterol	75.7mg
Sodium	874.9mg
Carbohydrates	31.0g
Protein	12.3g

Ingredients
2 hot dogs
2 hot dog buns
1 onion, halved and thinly sliced
1 tsp oil
1 tsp butter
1/2 tsp brown sugar

salt
pepper
3 oz. cream cheese

Directions
1. In a skillet, melt the butter and oil on medium-high heat and sauté the onion and sugar for about 20 minutes.
2. Season with the salt and pepper.
3. Meanwhile in another pan, add the cream cheese and heat soft and warm.
4. Cook the hot dogs according to the package's instructions.
5. Toast the buns.
6. Spread cream cheese over toasted buns and top with the hot dog and onions.

Hungry Bee
Hot Dogs

🥣 Prep Time: 10 mins

🕐 Total Time: 30 mins

Servings per Recipe: 12	
Calories	284.7
Fat	14.9g
Cholesterol	29.0mg
Sodium	735.7mg
Carbohydrates	26.4g
Protein	10.9g

Ingredients

8 hot dogs, chopped
4 oz. cheddar cheese, shredded
1 small onion, chopped
2 - 3 tbsp pickle relish
1 tsp prepared mustard

1 tsp ketchup
8 oz. chili
12 hot dog buns

Directions

1. Set your oven to 375 degrees F before doing anything else.
2. In a large bowl, add all the ingredients except buns and mix well.
3. Partially, remove the centers of the buns.
4. Fill each bun with the hot dog mixture.
5. Wrap each bun with a piece of foil and seal tightly.
6. Arrange the bun wraps onto a cookie sheet.
7. Cook in the oven for about 20 minutes.

LONDON
Sweet Onion Hot Dogs

Prep Time: 15 mins
Total Time: 15 mins

Servings per Recipe: 8
Calories   393.0
Fat   24.5g
Cholesterol   30.1mg
Sodium   1368.8mg
Carbohydrates   30.8g
Protein   11.3g

Ingredients

1 large sweet onion, finely chopped
2 minced garlic cloves
4 tbsp margarine
1/2 tsp salt
1/8 tsp pepper
1 1/2 tbsp prepared mustard
2 tbsp Worcestershire sauce
1 1/2 tsp white sugar

1/2 C. chili sauce
1 lb hot dog
8 hot dog buns

Directions

1. Set the broiler of your oven.
2. In a skillet, melt the margarine on medium-low heat and sauté the onion and garlic till tender.
3. Stir in the salt, pepper, Worcestershire, mustard, sugar and chili sauce and cook for about 5 minutes.
4. Split each hot dog lengthwise.
5. In a shallow pan, place the buns, split-side up.
6. Place the sauce over the hot dogs and cook under the broiler for about 3-5 minutes.
7. Serve with the extra sauce.

Fiesta
Hot Dogs

Prep Time: 10 mins
Total Time: 40 mins

Servings per Recipe: 10
Calories	405.6
Fat	28.1g
Cholesterol	54.0mg
Sodium	1436.4mg
Carbohydrates	24.6g
Protein	14.9g

Ingredients
10 hot dogs
1 (16 oz.) cans beans
1 tbsp prepared mustard

1 tbsp brown sugar
cheddar cheese

Directions
1. Set your oven to 350 degrees F before doing anything else and line a baking sheet with a greased piece of foil.
2. In a bowl, mix together the beans, mustard and sugar.
3. Cut the hot dogs lengthwise but not all the way through.
4. Open the hot dogs along the cut and arrange onto the prepared baking sheet.
5. Top with the bean mixture evenly.
6. Cook in the oven for about 30 minutes.
7. Remove the hot dogs from the oven and top with the cheese slices.
8. Cook in the oven till the cheese is melted.

BBQ
Hot Dog

Prep Time: 10 mins
Total Time: 17 mins

Servings per Recipe: 2
Calories	748.1
Fat	47.0g
Cholesterol	88.2mg
Sodium	1750.5mg
Carbohydrates	52.1g
Protein	28.0g

Ingredients

4 hot dogs
4 hot dog buns
4 -6 slices turkey bacon, fried and crumbled
1/2 C. Walla Walla onion, chopped
1/2 C. sharp cheddar cheese, shredded

1/2 C. tomatoes, diced
barbecue sauce
1 jalapeno pepper, seeded and diced (optional)

Directions

1. Cook the hot dogs on grill till desired doneness.
2. Toast the buns and top with the sauce, followed by the dog, cheese, bacon, onions and tomatoes.
3. Serve immediately.

Southwest
Hot Dogs

Prep Time: 10 mins
Total Time: 20 mins

Servings per Recipe: 1
Calories	569.2
Fat	35.6g
Cholesterol	67.7mg
Sodium	2029.9mg
Carbohydrates	41.2g
Protein	20.1g

Ingredients
1 beef hot dog
1 slice turkey bacon
1 bun (Mexican bouillon)
1 tbsp mustard
2 tbsp refried beans
2 tbsp guacamole
1/4 C. Mexican cheese, shredded

1/4 tomatoes, chopped and seeded
1/4 medium white onion, diced
2 tbsp salsa verde
1 tbsp mayonnaise, slightly thinned with lemon juice

Directions
1. Wrap the bacon slice around the hot dog.
2. Heat a nonstick skillet on medium-high heat and cook the hot dogs till crispy.
3. Cut the bouillon to create a pocket in the center but do not cut through the ends.
4. Spread the mustard over the bun, followed by the refried beans, guacamole, cheese, hot dog, tomato, onion, salsa verde and mayo.

AMERICAN
Hot Dogs

Prep Time: 10 mins
Total Time: 40 mins

Servings per Recipe: 10
Calories   349.2
Fat   20.4g
Cholesterol   34.4mg
Sodium   978.1mg
Carbohydrates   28.9g
Protein   12.0g

Ingredients
1 lb hot dog
10 hot dog buns
10 slices American cheese
10 tsp mayonnaise
20 tsp pickle relish

10 pieces aluminum foil (12 x 12 pieces)
ketchup (to taste)
mustard (to taste)

Directions
1. Set your oven to 350 degrees F before doing anything else.
2. Spread about 1 tsp of the mayonnaise over each hot dog bun and top with 1 slice of American cheese slice, followed by 1 hot dog and 2 tsp of the pickle relish.
3. Repeat with remaining buns and ingredients.
4. Wrap each hot dog combo in a piece of foil, crimping the ends and edges.
5. Cook in the oven for about 30 minutes.

Fort Collins
Hot Dogs

Prep Time: 10 mins
Total Time: 20 mins

Servings per Recipe: 4

Calories	330.1
Fat	20.0g
Cholesterol	33.0mg
Sodium	1070.4mg
Carbohydrates	25.5g
Protein	11.4g

Ingredients

1 tsp ketchup
1 tsp Dijon mustard
4 large hot dogs, knockwurst, or normal beef hot dogs
1/2 oz. cheddar cheese, cut into long sticks
2 tbsp chopped onions
1 C. refrigerated sauerkraut, squeeze to drain, roughly chopped
4 slices turkey bacon
vegetable oil
4 long hot dog buns

Directions

1. Set your grill for direct medium heat and lightly, grease the grill grate.
2. In a bowl, mix together the ketchup and mustard.
3. In another bowl, mix together the sauerkraut and chopped onion.
4. Split open the hot dogs, down the center, lengthwise, forming a deep pocket in each, but not cutting all the way through.
5. Coat the inside of each hot dog with the mustard ketchup mixture.
6. Arrange a cheese strip deep within each hot dog pocket and top with the sauerkraut and onions.
7. Encapsulate the cheese with the sauerkraut mixture at the ends as well, so that no cheese is exposed.
8. Wrap each stuffed hot dog with a bacon strip and secure with the toothpicks at each end.
9. Place the stuffed hot dogs on the grill, stuffing side down.
10. Cook the hot dogs, stuffing side down on the grill for about 2 minutes per side.
11. Flip the hot dogs a quarter turn and cook on grill for a couple of minutes, covering the grill in between and flipping.
12. During the last minute of cooking, open up the hot dog buns and place them open-side down on the grill till toasted lightly.
13. Transfer the hot dogs and buns onto a plate.
14. Remove the toothpicks from the hot dogs and arrange on the buns and serve.

HOT DOG
Pizza

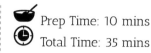

Prep Time: 10 mins
Total Time: 35 mins

Servings per Recipe: 3

Calories	2293.5
Fat	143.4g
Cholesterol	243.0mg
Sodium	5861.0mg
Carbohydrates	172.6g
Protein	73.9g

Ingredients
2 C. Bisquick
1/2 C. cold water
1 (7 1/2 oz.) cans canned chili
5 hot dogs, sliced thin
1 C. shredded cheddar cheese

Directions
1. In a bowl, add the Bisquick mix and water and mix till a soft dough forms.
2. Roll the dough into a 12-inch circle.
3. Arrange the dough circle onto an ungreased pizza pan and pinch the edges to form a crust.
4. Spread the chili over the crust and top with the cheese and hot dog slices.
5. Cook in the oven for about 20-25 minutes.

Northern Italian
Inspired Hot Dogs

Prep Time: 10 mins
Total Time: 25 mins

Servings per Recipe: 1
Calories	780.2
Fat	44.2g
Cholesterol	23.8mg
Sodium	841.5mg
Carbohydrates	81.6g
Protein	16.6g

Ingredients
1 hot dog
2 tbsp canola oil
1 medium potato
salt
pepper
1 small onion, sliced
1 green bell pepper

spicy mustard
1 torpedo roll (steak)

Directions
1. Cook the hot dogs on grill.
2. In a bowl, add the potato, oil, salt and pepper and toss to coat well.
3. In a skillet, sauté the potatoes till tender.
4. Add the onion and pepper and sauté till tender.
5. Arrange the hot dogs in torpedo roll and top with the spicy mustard, potatoes, peppers and onions.

MESA
Hot Dog Burritos

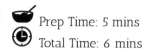

Prep Time: 5 mins
Total Time: 6 mins

Servings per Recipe: 4
Calories   278.4
Fat   17.2g
Cholesterol   229.3mg
Sodium   645.5mg
Carbohydrates   17.1g
Protein   12.5g

Ingredients
3 hot dogs
4 beaten eggs
sliced American cheese or cheddar cheese
4 flour tortillas

Directions
1. Cut the hot dogs in thin slices.
2. In a skillet, melt a little butter and cook the hot dogs slices till browned.
3. Stir in the beaten eggs and cook till scrambled.
4. Transfer the hot dog mixture into a microwave safe plate.
5. Top with the cheese slices and microwave for about 20 seconds.
6. Place all the ingredients in the flour tortillas and roll like a burrito.

South Carolina
Style Hot Dogs

Prep Time: 20 mins
Total Time: 4 hrs 20 mins

Servings per Recipe: 8
Calories	289.3
Fat	15.2g
Cholesterol	23.8mg
Sodium	806.0mg
Carbohydrates	27.5g
Protein	9.9g

Ingredients
8 all beef hot dogs
8 hot dog buns, steamed
3 C. shredded green cabbage
1 small carrot, grated
1/4 C. red onion, diced
1/4 C. sun-dried tomato, julienne cut
1 C. mayonnaise (light is fine)

1/4 C. red wine vinegar, plus
1 tbsp red wine vinegar
2 tbsp tomato ketchup
salt and pepper

Directions
1. For the dressing, in a small bowl mix together the mayonnaise and red wine vinegar.
2. In a large bowl, mix together the cabbage, carrot, red onion and sun dried tomatoes.
3. Add enough of the dressing and mix till the cabbage mixture moistens.
4. Add the ketchup and mix well.
5. Stir in the salt and pepper and refrigerate for about 4-5 hours.
6. Boil the hot dogs in boiling water and then drain.
7. Arrange 1 hot dog in steamed bun and top with the generous amounts of slaw.

WELCOME
to Weiner-Ville Hot Dogs

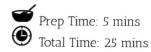 Prep Time: 5 mins

Total Time: 25 mins

Servings per Recipe: 5

Calories	344.4
Fat	18.1g
Cholesterol	19.0mg
Sodium	928.0mg
Carbohydrates	36.5g
Protein	10.4g

Ingredients
4 hot dogs
1/2 head cabbage, roughly chopped
1 medium onion, chopped
4 oz. tomato sauce
4 oz. salsa, chunky
1 tbsp sugar, granular
1/4 C. hot pepper, sliced
1 tsp hot pepper sauce

2 tbsp olive oil
5 hot dog buns
1/4 C. tap water

Directions
1. In a large no-stick skillet, heat the oil on medium heat and sauté all the
2. Ingredients except water for about 5 minutes.
3. Reduce the heat to medium-low and cook, covered for about 10-15 minutes. Stirring occasionally.
4. Place wiener pieces on a bun and top with the cooked cabbage and onions and top with a little mustard.

Summer
Safflower Fries

Prep Time: 10 mins
Total Time: 1 hr 10 mins

Servings per Recipe: 4
Calories   388 kcal
Fat   14.4 g
Carbohydrates   59.8g
Protein   6.6 g
Cholesterol   0 mg
Sodium   601 mg

Ingredients

cooking spray
6 Yukon Gold potatoes, cut into thick fries
1 tablespoon white sugar
1/4 cup Safflower oil
1 tsp tarragon
1 teaspoon garlic powder, or more to taste
1 teaspoon salt, or more to taste

1 teaspoon ground black pepper, or more to taste

Directions

1. Cover a casserole dish with foil the coat the foil with nonstick spray then set your oven to 425 degrees before doing anything else.
2. Get a colander for your potatoes and top them with the sugar evenly and toss. Let the potatoes sit for 40 mins to drain.
3. Get a bowl, combine: black pepper, tarragon, potatoes, Safflower oil, salt, and garlic powder.
4. Toss the potatoes evenly in the oil then layer them in the casserole dish evenly.
5. Cook everything in the oven for 25 mins then turn the fires and continue baking them for about 15 mins.
6. Enjoy.

COUNTRY
Cilantro Basil Rustic Sweet Potato Fries

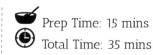

Prep Time: 15 mins
Total Time: 35 mins

Servings per Recipe: 2
Calories   299 kcal
Fat   9.7 g
Carbohydrates   46.2g
Protein   7.5 g
Cholesterol   9 mg
Sodium   439 mg

Ingredients

2 sweet potatoes, cut into French fries
1 tablespoon olive oil
1/4 cup Parmesan cheese
2 tablespoons chopped fresh cilantro
1 tbsp fresh basil, chopped
sea salt and ground black pepper to taste

Directions

1. Set your oven to 425 degrees before doing anything else.
2. Get bowl, combine: olive oil, and sweet potatoes. Stir everything completely then layer the potatoes in a casserole dish.
3. Cook the fries in the oven for 14 mins then then flip them and continue to cooking them for about another 10 mins.
4. Place everything into a serving bowl and top the fries, while they are still hot with the parmesan, basil, and cilantro. Toss everything then add the salt, toss again then add the pepper.
5. Enjoy.

July 4th
Mustard Pepper Lime Fries

Prep Time: 10 mins
Total Time: 40 mins

Servings per Recipe: 4

Calories	269 kcal
Fat	11 g
Carbohydrates	39.6g
Protein	5 g
Cholesterol	0 mg
Sodium	699 mg

Ingredients

4 russet potatoes, peeled and cut into 1/4 inch thick fries
3 tablespoons olive oil
2 tablespoons lime juice
2 cloves garlic, minced
1/2 teaspoon red pepper flakes
1/4 teaspoon cayenne pepper

1 teaspoon chili powder
2 tablespoons spicy brown mustard
1/2 teaspoon ground black pepper
1 teaspoon salt

Directions

1. Set your oven to 400 degrees before doing anything else.
2. Get a bowl, combine: pepper, olive oil, mustard, lime juice, chili powder, and garlic, cayenne, and pepper flakes. Stir the spices then add in the potatoes and toss everything nicely.
3. Place the fries in a jelly roll pan that has been greased lightly or coated with non-stick spray and cook everything in the oven for 18 mins. Flip the potatoes and continue cooking for 14 more mins or until the potatoes are completely done.
4. Enjoy after topping the fries with salt.

BUTTER LEMON
Pepper French Fries

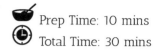 Prep Time: 10 mins

Total Time: 30 mins

Servings per Recipe: 8

Calories	227 kcal
Fat	11.3 g
Carbohydrates	29.9 g
Protein	3 g
Cholesterol	15 mg
Sodium	849 mg

Ingredients

1 32 ounce package frozen French fries
2 1/2 tablespoons lemon pepper
2 tablespoons dried red pepper seasoning
1 tablespoon garlic powder
black pepper to taste

2 pinches chili powder
1/4 cup butter

Directions

1. Set your oven to 425 degrees before doing anything else.
2. Coat a baking dish with some nonstick spray then place your potatoes in the dish. Top the potatoes with: chili powder, lemon pepper, garlic powder, red pepper. Toss everything then dot the fries with the butter evenly.
3. Cook everything in the oven for 17 mins flipping the potatoes half way. If the fries are not done cook them for about 7 more mins.
4. Enjoy.

Copycat
Fast Food Franchise Fries

🥣 Prep Time: 10 mins
🕐 Total Time: 1 h 15 mins

Servings per Recipe: 4
Calories   600 kcal
Fat   322.4 g
Carbohydrates   394.8g
Protein   38.6 g
Cholesterol   0 mg
Sodium   112 mg

Ingredients

8 potatoes, peeled and cut into 1/4-inch thick fries
1/4 cup white sugar
2 tablespoons corn syrup
1 quart canola oil, or as needed

boiling water
sea salt to taste

Directions

1. Get a bowl, for your potatoes and let them sit submerged in water for 15 mins then remove the liquid and dry the potatoes.
2. Now submerge the potatoes in just enough boiling water then add in the corn syrup and sugar and stir everything. Do this in a metal bowl. Put everything in the fridge for 10 mins. Remove the liquid and dry the potatoes with some paper towels.
3. Get a casserole dish or jelly roll pan and lay out the fries on the dish, place a covering plastic on the dish and put everything in the freezer for 45 mins.
4. Now get your oil hot for frying to about 350 to 360 degrees and once the oil is hot begin to 1.3 of the fries in the oil for 3 mins. Place the fries on a plate with some paper towel to drain and let them for about 10 mins. Continue to work in batches until all the fries are done.
5. Now re fry the fries a second time 1/3 at a time for 6 mins each batch then season the fries with some salt.
6. Enjoy.

FRENCH SEASONED
Fries with Tourtiere

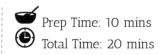

Prep Time: 10 mins
Total Time: 20 mins

Servings per Recipe: 8	
Calories	192 kcal
Fat	3.1 g
Carbohydrates	37.8g
Protein	3.9 g
Cholesterol	0 mg
Sodium	751 mg

Ingredients

2 1/2 pounds russet potatoes, peeled, cut into matchsticks, soaked in cold water
1 cup all-purpose flour
1 teaspoon garlic salt
1 teaspoon onion salt
1 tsp Tourtiere spice mix

1 teaspoon salt
1 teaspoon paprika
1/2 cup water, or as needed
1 cup vegetable oil for frying

Directions

1. Get your oil hot in a frying pan.

2. As the oil heats begin to sift the following spices into a bowl: paprika, Tourtiere, flour, salt, garlic salt, and onion salt. Add in a small amount of water to make the spice mix slightly battery just enough so that it would drip from a utensils.

3. Coat your fries evenly with batter carefully then carefully place them into the hot oil. Make sure you lay each fry into the oil separately so as to avoid any sticking together.

4. Let the fry cook until they are golden.

NOTE: For the tourtiere spice mix combine the following and crush. Then store in a container for later use: 1 tsp celery salt, 1/2 tsp ground black pepper, 1/2 tsp crushed savory, 1/2 tsp ground cloves, 1/2 tsp ground cinnamon, 1/2 tsp ground thyme, 1/4 tsp ground sage, 1/4 tsp mustard powder

Loaded
State Fair Fries

Prep Time: 5 mins
Total Time: 25 mins

Servings per Recipe: 6
Calories	509 kcal
Fat	25.2 g
Carbohydrates	351.6g
Protein	19.8 g
Cholesterol	449 mg
Sodium	1484 mg

Ingredients

1 32 ounce package frozen seasoned French fries
2 tablespoons cornstarch
2 tablespoons water
2 cups low-fat milk
1 tablespoon margarine
8 slices American cheese, cut into pieces

1 15 ounce can chili without beans such as Hormel, or vegetarian chili for meatless

Directions

1. Cook your fries in the oven for about 25 mins until they are golden brown at 350 degrees.
2. Get a small bowl and combine your water and cornstarch evenly.
3. Get a saucepan with the margarine and milk boiling while whisking then set the heat to low and stir in the cornstarch mix into the milk mix. Set the heat to a medium level and continue heat the mix until it becomes thick while stirring.
4. Combine in the cheese slices and stir the mix until everything is melted. Then heat your chili in a separate pot.
5. Once the milk mix is done and the chili as well top your fries with the chili and cheese and serve.
6. Enjoy.

Loaded State Fair Fries

67

RUSTIC
Windmill Fries

Prep Time: 20 mins
Total Time: 50 mins

Servings per Recipe: 2

Calories	310 kcal
Fat	12.8 g
Carbohydrates	45.5g
Protein	5.4 g
Cholesterol	15 mg
Sodium	497 mg

Ingredients
4 medium Yukon Gold potatoes, wedges
1 tablespoon butter
1 tablespoon olive oil, or more to taste
2 cloves garlic, minced
1/2 teaspoon Fine Sea Salt
1 teaspoon ground black pepper

Directions
1. Set your oven to 400 degrees before doing anything else.
2. Get your garlic, olive oil, and butter heating in a pot then combine in the salt and pepper. Stir everything evenly then coat the wedges evenly with the garlic sauce.
3. Place everything into a casserole dish evenly dispersed and for 40 mins cook the fries in the oven.
4. Enjoy.

Saint Francis's
Feast Fries

Prep Time: 5 mins
Total Time: 30 mins

Servings per Recipe: 4
Calories	99 kcal
Fat	3.6 g
Carbohydrates	15.9g
Protein	1.6 g
Cholesterol	0 mg
Sodium	153 mg

Ingredients
olive oil cooking spray
4 russet potatoes
1 tablespoon olive oil
1 tablespoon chopped fresh rosemary
1 1/2 teaspoons dried thyme leaves
1 teaspoon garlic powder
1/2 teaspoon dried oregano leaves

1/2 teaspoon dried parsley
1/2 teaspoon ground sage
1/2 teaspoon cracked black pepper
1/4 teaspoon salt

Directions
1. Coat a casserole dish or jelly roll pan with nonstick spray then set your oven to 425 degrees before doing anything else.
2. Get a bowl for your potatoes and place a towel over the bowl or some plastic wrap and cook everything in the microwave for 5 mins with a high level of heat. Let the potatoes lose their heat then slice each one into wedges.
3. Get a 2nd bowl for your cut potatoes and coat them with the olive oil and toss them. Layer the potatoes on the jelly roll pan or casserole dish and cook them with the oven for 12 mins then coat them some nonstick spray and cook them for 14 more mins.
4. Get a small dish and combine: salt, rosemary, pepper, thyme, sage, parsley, garlic powder, and oregano.
5. Top your potatoes with the spice mix while they are still hot and toss them.
6. Enjoy.

CURRIED
Picnic Fries

🍲 Prep Time: 10 mins
🕐 Total Time: 30 mins

Servings per Recipe: 8
Calories	162 kcal
Fat	4.1 g
Carbohydrates	28.5g
Protein	3.8 g
Cholesterol	< 1 mg
Sodium	< 322 mg

Ingredients
6 potatoes, cut into wedges
2 tablespoons vegetable oil
2 tablespoons shredded Parmesan cheese
2 teaspoons curry powder
1 teaspoon paprika

1 teaspoon salt
1/2 teaspoon garlic powder

Directions
1. Set your oven to 400 degrees before doing anything else.
2. Coat a jelly roll pan with nonstick spray.
3. Get a bowl, combine: garlic powder, veggie oil, salt, parmesan, paprika, and curry. Toss everything evenly to coat the potatoes layer everything into the pan.
4. Cook the wedges in the oven for about 14 mins then flip them and continue cooking for 10 more mins.
5. Enjoy.

Chipotle
Coleslaw

🥣 Prep Time: 30 mins

🕐 Total Time: 30 mins

Servings per Recipe: 8

Calories	41 kcal
Fat	0.3 g
Carbohydrates	< 9.3g
Protein	1.6 g
Cholesterol	0 mg
Sodium	73 mg

Ingredients
4 C. chopped or shredded cabbage
1 medium red bell pepper, chopped
1 C. thinly sliced green onions
1 C. cooked corn kernels
1/2 C. rice vinegar
1/3 C. Splenda no-calorie sweetener
Salt and pepper, to taste (optional)

1 tbsp finely minced jalapeno pepper, seeds and veins removed (optional)
1/2 C. chopped cilantro (optional)

Directions
1. Toss all ingredients together.
2. In a bowl, add all the ingredients and toss to coat well.

BALTIMORE
Style Coleslaw

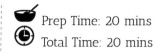

Prep Time: 20 mins

Total Time: 20 mins

Servings per Recipe: 8

Calories	115 kcal
Fat	11 g
Carbohydrates	4.2g
Protein	0.6 g
Cholesterol	5 mg
Sodium	152 mg

Ingredients
1/2 C. mayonnaise
2 tbsp chopped onion
1 tbsp vinegar
2 tsp white sugar
1 tsp seafood seasoning (such as Old Bay(R))

3 C. shredded cabbage
1/2 C. shredded carrots
1/4 C. chopped green bell pepper

Directions
1. In a large salad bowl, add the mayonnaise, onion, vinegar, sugar and seafood seasoning and beat till the sugar is dissolved.
2. Add the cabbage, carrots and green bell pepper and stir to combine well.

Hot Cross
Coleslaw

Prep Time: 30 mins
Total Time: 2 h 15 mins

Servings per Recipe: 6
Calories   109 kcal
Fat   7.2 g
Carbohydrates   11.1g
Protein   0.9 g
Cholesterol   0 mg
Sodium   125 mg

Ingredients

3 tbsp apple cider vinegar
3 tbsp canola oil
3 tbsp white sugar
1/4 tsp dry mustard
1/4 tsp poppy seeds
1/4 tsp ground black pepper
1/4 tsp salt

1/4 tsp hot pepper sauce (optional)
4 C. shredded green cabbage
2 carrots, shredded

Directions

1. In a bowl, add the apple cider vinegar, canola oil, sugar, dry mustard, poppy seeds, black pepper, salt and hot pepper and mix till the sugar is dissolved.
2. In a large salad bowl, mix together the cabbage and carrots.
3. Place the dressing over the slaw and stir to coat.
4. Refrigerate for at least 2 hours before serving.

THOUSAND ISLAND
Coleslaw

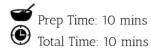

Prep Time: 10 mins
Total Time: 10 mins

Servings per Recipe: 6

Calories	27 kcal
Fat	2 g
Carbohydrates	2.5g
Protein	< 0.1 g
Cholesterol	< 2 mg
Sodium	< 242 mg

Ingredients
1 (10 oz.) package angel hair-style
shredded cabbage
2 tbsp Thousand Island dressing
2 tbsp seasoned rice vinegar
1 tsp hot sauce
1 pinch salt

Directions
1. In a bowl, add the cabbage, Thousand Island dressing, rice vinegar, hot sauce and with a fork, mix till well combined.

Creamy
Central Coleslaw

🥣 Prep Time: 15 mins
🕐 Total Time: 2 h 15 mins

Servings per Recipe: 8
Calories	160 kcal
Fat	11.4 g
Carbohydrates	14.6g
Protein	1.3 g
Cholesterol	6 mg
Sodium	103 mg

Ingredients
1/2 C. mayonnaise
1/3 C. white sugar
1/4 C. milk
2 tbsp lemon juice
1 1/2 tbsp white vinegar
2 tsp sour cream
1/2 tsp freshly ground black pepper

1 pinch cayenne pepper, or to taste
1 lb. cabbage, cut into wedges
2 carrots
1/4 small onion, chopped

Directions
1. In a bowl, add the mayonnaise, sugar, milk, lemon juice, vinegar, sour cream, black pepper and cayenne pepper and mix till well combined.
2. In a food processor, add the cabbage, carrots and onion and with a grater attachment, shred them.
3. Transfer the vegetables mixture in a large bowl.
4. Add the mayonnaise mixture and stir to combine.
5. Refrigerate, covered for at least 2 hours or overnight.
6. Stir coleslaw before serving.

BAVARIAN
Style Coleslaw

Prep Time: 10 mins
Total Time: 2 hr 10 mins

Servings per Recipe: 6

Calories	183 kcal
Fat	14.7 g
Carbohydrates	12.7g
Protein	1.5 g
Cholesterol	7 mg
Sodium	316 mg

Ingredients
1/2 head cabbage, thinly sliced
3 tbsp white sugar
3 tbsp cider vinegar
1/2 tsp celery seed
1/2 tsp salt
1/2 C. mayonnaise

Directions
1. In a large bowl, place the cabbage.
2. In another bowl, mix together the sugar, vinegar, celery seed and salt.
3. Add the mayonnaise and mix till dressing is smooth and creamy.
4. Place the dressing over the cabbage and toss to coat.
5. Refrigerator for about 2-3 hours.
6. Stir well before serving.

Picnic
Coleslaw

Prep Time: 10 mins
Total Time: 10 mins

Servings per Recipe: 12
Calories	209 kcal
Fat	16.8 g
Carbohydrates	13.6g
Protein	1.7 g
Cholesterol	13 mg
Sodium	294 mg

Ingredients
1 (16 oz.) package shredded coleslaw mix
2 C. seedless red grapes, halved
1/2 C. shredded carrot
1 C. mayonnaise
1/4 C. prepared Dijon-style mustard

1/3 C. crumbled blue cheese
2 tbsp white sugar
2 tbsp cider vinegar

Directions
1. In a large bowl, add mayonnaise, mustard, cheese, sugar and vinegar and beat till well combined.
2. Add the coleslaw mix, grapes and carrots and stir till well combined.
3. Refrigerate to chill before serving.

ALABAMA
Inspired Coleslaw

Prep Time: 20 mins
Total Time: 2 hr 20 mins

Servings per Recipe: 8
Calories	184 kcal
Fat	11.3 g
Carbohydrates	20.3g
Protein	2.7 g
Cholesterol	6 mg
Sodium	274 mg

Ingredients
1 head cabbage, finely shredded
2 carrots, finely chopped
2 tbsp finely chopped onion
1/2 C. mayonnaise
1/3 C. white sugar
1/4 C. milk
1/4 C. buttermilk
2 tbsp lemon juice

2 tbsp distilled white vinegar
1/2 tsp salt
1/8 tsp ground black pepper

Directions
1. In a large salad bowl, mix together the cabbage, carrots and onion.
2. In another bowl, add the mayonnaise, sugar, milk, buttermilk, lemon juice, vinegar, salt and black pepper and beat till smooth and the sugar is dissolved.
3. Place the dressing over cabbage mixture and mix till well combined.
4. Refrigerate, covered for at least 2 hours.
5. Just before serving, mix again before serving.

Rice Vinegar and Lime Coleslaw

Prep Time: 25 mins
Total Time: 25 mins

Servings per Recipe: 7
Calories   189 kcal
Fat   18.8 g
Carbohydrates   5.6g
Protein   0.9 g
Cholesterol   9 mg
Sodium   164 mg

Ingredients

3/4 C. mayonnaise
1 lime, zested
2 tsp fresh lime juice
1/2 tsp rice vinegar
2 cloves garlic, minced
2 tsp sweet chili sauce
2 tsp white sugar

3 tbsp finely chopped fresh cilantro
1/4 red onion, finely diced
4 C. shredded green cabbage

Directions

1. In a large bowl, add the mayonnaise, lime zest, lime juice, rice vinegar, garlic, sweet chili sauce and sugar and mix till the sugar dissolves.
2. Add the cilantro and red onion and stir to combine.
3. Slowly, add the cabbage about 1 C. at a time, mixing till all the cabbage is coated.

SPICY
Fried Chicken Wings 101

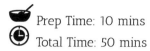 Prep Time: 10 mins

Total Time: 50 mins

Servings per Recipe: 6

Calories	531 kcal
Fat	41.3 g
Carbohydrates	25.1g
Protein	15.8 g
Cholesterol	37 mg
Sodium	1768 mg

Ingredients

12 small chicken wings
1/4 tsp seasoned salt, or to taste
1 C. all-purpose flour
1 tsp coarse salt
1/2 tsp ground black pepper
1/4 tsp cayenne pepper
1/4 tsp paprika

1 (12 fluid oz.) bottle Buffalo wing sauce
2 quarts vegetable oil for frying

Directions

1. Sprinkle the chicken wings with the seasoned salt evenly.
2. In a shallow dish, mix together the flour, paprika, cayenne pepper, salt and black pepper.
3. Cover and refrigerate to marinate for about 15-30 minutes.
4. In a large skillet, heat the oil to 375 degrees F and fry the chicken wings for about 10 minutes on both sides.
5. Transfer the chicken onto paper towel lined plates to drain.

Messy
Oven Fried Picnic Chicken

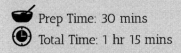

Prep Time: 30 mins
Total Time: 1 hr 15 mins

Servings per Recipe: 7
Calories	690 kcal
Fat	53.2 g
Carbohydrates	17.9g
Protein	34.1 g
Cholesterol	114 mg
Sodium	967 mg

Ingredients

1 (2 to 3 lb.) whole chicken, cut into pieces
1 C. dried bread crumbs
1 tsp garlic powder
1 tsp salt

1 tsp ground black pepper
1 tsp dried thyme
1/2 tsp paprika
1 C. mayonnaise

Directions

1. Set your oven to 350 degrees F before doing anything else and lightly, grease a 13x9-inch baking dish.
2. In a shallow dish, mix together the flour, paprika, cayenne pepper, salt and black pepper and mix well.
3. Add the chicken pieces and coat the meat with the mixture generously.
4. Arrange the chicken pieces onto the prepared baking sheet in a single layer.
5. Cook everything in the oven for about 45 minutes.

MARIA'S
Buttermilk Chicken

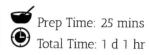
Prep Time: 25 mins
Total Time: 1 d 1 hr

Servings per Recipe: 7
Calories	990 kcal
Fat	82.7 g
Carbohydrates	133.2g
Protein	29.4 g
Cholesterol	98 mg
Sodium	567 mg

Ingredients
1 (3 lb.) whole chicken, cut into pieces
2 C. buttermilk
1 C. dry potato flakes
1 C. all-purpose flour
1 tsp poultry seasoning

1/2 tsp salt
1 tsp freshly ground black pepper
2 C. vegetable oil for frying

Directions
1. In a shallow dish, mix together the chicken pieces and buttermilk.
2. Cover and refrigerate to marinate overnight
3. In another shallow dish, mix together all the remaining ingredients.
4. Remove the chicken pieces from the buttermilk and coat them with the flour mixture evenly and keep aside for about 15 minutes.
5. In a large skillet, heat the oil to 350 degrees F and fry the chicken pieces till golden brown completely.
6. Transfer the chicken onto paper towel lined plates to drain.

Chicken Tenders 101 w/ Spicy Dipping Sauce

Prep Time: 30 mins
Total Time: 1 hr

Servings per Recipe: 8
Calories	821 kcal
Fat	55.2 g
Carbohydrates	35.2g
Protein	45.2 g
Cholesterol	164 mg
Sodium	783 mg

Ingredients

1 C. all-purpose flour
2 C. Italian-style seasoned bread crumbs
1/2 tsp ground black pepper
1/2 tsp cayenne pepper
2 eggs, beaten
2 tbsp water
24 chicken tenderloins

2 quarts oil for frying
1 C. mayonnaise
3 tbsp prepared horseradish
1/2 C. sour cream
1 dash Worcestershire sauce
3 tbsp prepared mustard

Directions

1. In a shallow dish, place the flour.
2. In a second shallow dish, beat together the water and eggs.
3. In a third shallow dish, mix together the breadcrumbs, cayenne pepper and black pepper.
4. First coat the chicken tenderloins in the flour, followed by the egg mixture and the breadcrumb mixture.
5. In a large skillet, heat the oil to 375 degrees F and fry the chicken tenderloins for about 6-8 minutes.
6. Meanwhile for the dipping sauce, in a bowl, mix together the remaining ingredients.
7. Transfer the chicken onto paper towel lined plates to drain.
8. Serve the chicken with the dipping sauce.

THE PERFECT
Gluten-Free Chicken Cutlet

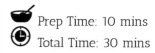

Prep Time: 10 mins
Total Time: 30 mins

Servings per Recipe: 6
Calories	261 kcal
Fat	12.2 g
Carbohydrates	1.8g
Protein	34.2 g
Cholesterol	93 mg
Sodium	446 mg

Ingredients
2 C. oil
1 C. gluten-free all-purpose flour
2 tsp powdered buttermilk
1 tsp paprika
1 tsp celery salt
1/2 tsp ground white pepper

1/2 tsp xanthan gum
1/2 tsp baking soda
1/4 tsp cayenne pepper
2 lb. skinless, boneless chicken breast halves

Directions
1. In a large shallow dish, mix together all the ingredients except the chicken breast halves and the oil.
2. Add the chicken breast halves and coat them with the mixture generously.
3. In a large skillet, heat the oil to 375 degrees F and fry the chicken tenderloins for about 5 minutes per side.
4. Transfer the chicken onto paper towel lined plates to drain.

Memphis Inspired
Fried Chicken Breast

🥣 Prep Time: 30 mins

🕐 Total Time: 8 h 35 mins

Servings per Recipe: 8

Calories	635 kcal
Fat	22.7 g
Carbohydrates	69.4g
Protein	37.1 g
Cholesterol	258 mg
Sodium	3112 mg

Ingredients

8 skinless, boneless chicken breast halves, pounded to 3/4-inch thickness
1 quart buttermilk
3 shallots, finely chopped
2 tbsp chopped garlic
2 tbsp salt
2 tbsp white sugar

1 1/4 tsp ground cumin
1 1/2 tsp ground black pepper
2 C. vegetable oil for frying
4 C. all-purpose flour
2 tbsp baking powder
2 tsp salt
8 large eggs, beaten

Directions

1. In a resealable bag, mix together the buttermilk, garlic, shallots, sugar, cumin, salt and black pepper.
2. Add the chicken breast halves and tightly, seal the bag and shake to coat well.
3. Refrigerate to marinate overnight.
4. In a shallow dish, mix together the flour, baking powder and salt.
5. In another shallow dish, add the eggs.
6. Remove the chicken breast halves from the refrigerator and shake off the excess marinade.
7. First, coat the chicken breast halves in the flour mixture, then dip everything into the eggs and again coat them with the flour mixture.
8. In a large skillet, heat the oil on medium heat and fry the chicken breasts halves for about 2-3 minutes per side.
9. Transfer the chicken onto paper towel lined plates to drain.

5 STAR
Fried Chicken

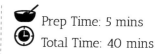

Prep Time: 5 mins
Total Time: 40 mins

Servings per Recipe: 7
Calories   740 kcal
Fat   45.4 g
Carbohydrates   25.1g
Protein   53.8 g
Cholesterol   1250 mg
Sodium   767 mg

Ingredients
2 eggs, beaten
2/3 C. milk
1 1/2 C. all-purpose flour
1 (.7 oz.) package dry Italian-style salad
dressing mix

1 packet dry tomato soup mix
1 (4 lb.) whole chicken, cut into pieces
2 tbsp vegetable oil

Directions
1. In a shallow dish, beat together the eggs and milk.
2. In another dish, mix together the remaining ingredients except the chicken and the oil.
3. Dip the chicken pieces in the egg mixture and roll them in the flour mixture evenly.
4. In a large skillet, heat the oil on medium-high heat and fry the chicken pieces for about 25-35 minutes, flipping occasionally.
5. Transfer the chicken onto paper towel lined plates to drain.

Curry
Fried Chicken

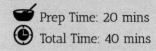

Prep Time: 20 mins
Total Time: 40 mins

Servings per Recipe: 2
Calories	313 kcal
Fat	16.1 g
Carbohydrates	20.1g
Protein	22.1 g
Cholesterol	45 mg
Sodium	1214 mg

Ingredients

6 tbsp skinless, boneless chicken breast, cut into small pieces
2 tbsp soy sauce
2 tbsp dry sherry
1 tbsp cornstarch
1 tbsp vegetable oil
1 C. broccoli florets, cut into pieces

1 large green bell pepper, cut into squares
1 zucchini, cut into rounds and quartered
3 cloves garlic, minced
1/2 C. chicken broth
1 tbsp vegetable oil
6 green onions, chopped

Directions

1. In a large bowl, mix together the chicken, sherry, soy sauce and cornstarch.
2. In a large skillet, heat 1 tbsp of the oil on medium-high heat and stir fry the vegetables and garlic for about 2-3 minutes.
3. Stir in the broth and simmer, covered for about 4-5 minutes.
4. Transfer the vegetable mixture in a bowl and keep aside.
5. With a paper towel, wipe out the skillet.
6. In the same skillet, heat the remaining oil on medium-high heat and stir fry the chicken for about 5 minutes.
7. Add the vegetable mixture and stir fry the chicken for about 2-3 minutes.
8. Serve with a garnishing of green onions.

SPICED
Chicken

🍲 Prep Time: 15 mins
🕐 Total Time: 20 mins

Servings per Recipe: 5
Calories	177 kcal
Fat	7.1 g
Carbohydrates	5.2g
Protein	21.9 g
Cholesterol	53 mg
Sodium	102 mg

Ingredients

2 tbsp vegetable oil
1 lb. skinless, boneless chicken breast halves
1 onion, sliced
1 tsp ginger garlic paste
2 green chili peppers, chopped
3 tsp ground coriander seed
1 tsp garam masala
1/2 tsp ground turmeric

1 tsp chili powder
1 pinch ground nutmeg
1 tbsp fresh chopped cilantro, for garnish
salt to taste

Directions

1. In a pan, heat the oil and stir fry the green chili pepper, onion, ginger-garlic paste and garam masala powder till the onion becomes golden brown.
2. Stir in the chicken pieces, nutmeg, chili powder, turmeric and black pepper and stir fry it for about 5-6 minutes.
3. Stir in the coriander powder and salt and fry it till the desired doneness.
4. Serve with a garnishing of cilantro.

Easy Mexican
Fried Chicken Chimichangas

🥣 Prep Time: 20 mins
🕐 Total Time: 45 mins

Servings per Recipe: 1
Calories	353.9
Fat	16.8g
Cholesterol	46.0mg7
Sodium	17.8mg
Carbohydrates	31.4g
Protein	18.7g

Ingredients

2/3 C. your favorite salsa
1 tsp ground cumin
1/2 tsp dried oregano leaves, crushed
1 1/2 C. cooked chicken, chopped
1 C. shredded cheddar cheese
2 green onions, chopped with some tops
6 (8 inch) flour tortillas

2 tbsp margarine, melted
shredded cheddar cheese, for serving
chopped green onion, for serving
picante sauce, for serving

Directions

1. Set your oven to 400 degrees F before doing anything else.
2. In a bowl, mix together the chicken, salsa, cheese, green onions, oregano and cumin.
3. Divide about 1/4 C. of the chicken mixture in the center of the each tortilla.
4. Roll each tortilla to seal the filling.
5. Arrange the rolls onto a baking sheet in a single layer, seam-side down and coat with the melted margarine evenly.
6. Cook everything in the oven for about 25 minutes.
7. Serve with a garnishing of cheese and green onion alongside the remaining chicken mixture.

AMERICAN
Potato Salad

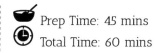
Prep Time: 45 mins
Total Time: 60 mins

Servings per Recipe: 8
Calories	206 kcal
Fat	7.6 g
Carbohydrates	30.5g
Protein	5.5 g
Cholesterol	72 mg
Sodium	335 mg

Ingredients
5 potatoes
3 eggs
1 C. diced celery
1/2 C. diced onion
1/2 C. sweet pickle relish
1/4 tsp garlic salt
1/4 tsp celery salt

1 tbsp prepared mustard
ground black pepper to taste
1/4 C. mayonnaise

Directions
1. Boil your potatoes in water and salt for 20 mins. Then remove the skins and chunk them.
2. Now get your eggs boiling in water.
3. Once the water is boiling, place a lid on the pot, and shut the heat.
4. Let the eggs sit for 15 mins. Then once they have cooled remove the shells, and dice them.
5. Get a bowl, combine: mayo, potatoes, pepper, eggs, mustard, celery, celery salt, onions, garlic, and relish.
6. Place a covering of plastic on the mix and put everything in the fridge until it is cold.
7. Enjoy.

Egg
Salad

 Prep Time: 10 mins

Total Time: 35 mins

Servings per Recipe: 4

Calories	344 kcal
Fat	31.9 g
Carbohydrates	2.3g
Protein	< 13 g
Cholesterol	382 mg
Sodium	1351 mg

Ingredients
8 eggs
1/2 C. mayonnaise
1 tsp prepared yellow mustard

1/4 C. diced green onion
salt and pepper to taste
1/4 tsp paprika

Directions
1. Boil your eggs in water for 2 mins then place a lid on the pot and let the contents sit for 15 mins. Once the eggs have cooled remove their shells and dice them.
2. Now get a bowl, combine: green onions, eggs, mustard, and mayo.
3. Stir the mix until it is smooth then add in the paprika, pepper, and salt.
4. Stir the contents again then enjoy with toasted buns.

CHICKEN
Salad

Prep Time: 15 mins
Total Time: 20 mins

Servings per Recipe: 12
Calories	315 kcal
Fat	23.1 g
Carbohydrates	15.2g
Protein	13.9 g
Cholesterol	42 mg
Sodium	213 mg

Ingredients

4 C. cubed, cooked chicken meat
1 C. mayonnaise
1 tsp paprika
1 1/2 C. dried cranberries
1 C. diced celery
2 green onions, diced

1/2 C. minced green bell pepper
1 C. diced pecans
1 tsp seasoning salt
ground black pepper to taste

Directions

1. Get a bowl, combine: seasoned salt, paprika, and mayo. Get this mix smooth then add in: the nuts, celery, onion, bell peppers, and cranberries.
2. Mix everything again then add the chicken and black pepper.
3. Place the contents in the fridge for 65 mins then serve.
4. Enjoy.

Corn Salad

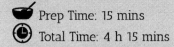 Prep Time: 15 mins

Total Time: 4 h 15 mins

Servings per Recipe: 8

Calories	201 kcal
Fat	13.3 g
Carbohydrates	18g
Protein	2.4 g
Cholesterol	5 mg
Sodium	340 mg

Ingredients

Dressing:
1/2 cup mayonnaise
3 small green onions, thinly sliced
2 tablespoons white wine vinegar
2 tablespoons minced pickled jalapeno peppers
2 tablespoons minced fresh parsley

1 tablespoon light olive oil
salt and ground black pepper to taste
Vegetables:
2 (11 ounce) cans shoepeg corn, rinsed and drained
1 cup halved grape tomatoes

Directions

1. Get a bowl, combine: olive oil, mayo, parsley, green onion, jalapeno, and vinegar. Work the mix completely then combine in some pepper and salt.
2. Now stir in your tomatoes and corn into the mayo mix. Place a covering of plastic on the bowl and put everything in the fridge for 4 hours.
3. Enjoy.

ENSALADA
de Papas Colombiana
(10-Ingredient Potato Salad)

Prep Time: 20 mins
Total Time: 40 mins

Servings per Recipe: 8
Calories	124.1
Fat	2.0g
Cholesterol	0.0mg
Sodium	43.1mg
Carbohydrates	24.8g
Protein	3.1g

Ingredients

2 lb. red potatoes, cooked, peeled and cut into 1-inch cubes when cool
3 large carrots, peeled, cut into 1/2-inch pieces and steamed until crisp-tender, cooled
1/2 C. chopped red onion
1/4-1/2 C. chopped cilantro, depending on taste

3 large tomatoes, cut into 1-inch chunks
Salad Dressing
1/3 C. wine vinegar
1 tbsp oil
1 tsp seasoning salt (may add more to taste)
1 tsp sugar
1/4 tsp fresh ground black pepper

Directions

1. In a large bowl, mix together the potato cubes, carrot pieces, chopped onions and cilantro.
2. In a small bowl, add all the dressing ingredients and beat till well combined.
3. Place the dressing over the salad with the tomato chunks and gently, stir to combine.
4. Refrigerate to chill before serving.

Tuna
Salad

Prep Time: 10 mins
Total Time: 10 mins

Servings per Recipe: 4

Calories	228 kcal
Fat	17.3 g
Carbohydrates	5.3g
Protein	13.4 g
Cholesterol	24 mg
Sodium	255 mg

Ingredients

1 (7 oz.) can white tuna, drained and
flaked
6 tbsps mayonnaise or salad dressing
1 tbsp Parmesan cheese
3 tbsps sweet pickle relish
1/8 tsp dried minced onion flakes
1/4 tsp curry powder

1 tbsp dried parsley
1 tsp dried dill weed
1 pinch garlic powder

Directions

1. Get a bowl, combine: onion flakes, tuna, parmesan, and mayo.
2. Stir the contents until they are smooth then add the garlic powder, curry powder, dill, and parsley.
3. Stir the contents again to evenly distribute the spices.
4. Enjoy over toasted buns or crackers.

MACARONI
Salad

Prep Time: 20 mins
Total Time: 4 h 30 mins

Servings per Recipe: 10
Calories   390 kcal
Fat   18.7 g
Carbohydrates   49.3g
Protein   6.8 g
Cholesterol   8 mg
Sodium   529 mg

Ingredients

4 C. uncooked elbow macaroni
1 C. mayonnaise
1/4 C. distilled white vinegar
2/3 C. white sugar
2 1/2 tbsps prepared yellow mustard
1 1/2 tsps salt
1/2 tsp ground black pepper

1 large onion, diced
2 stalks celery, diced
1 green bell pepper, seeded and diced
1/4 C. grated carrot
2 tbsps diced pimento peppers

Directions

1. Boil your macaroni in water and salt for 9 mins then remove the liquids.
2. Get a bowl, combine: macaroni, onions, pimentos, celery, carrots, black pepper, mayo, salt, green peppers, vinegar, mustard, and sugar.
3. Place a covering of plastic around the bowl and put everything in the fridge for 5 hrs.
4. Enjoy.

Mesa
Macaroni Salad

Prep Time: 10 mins
Total Time: 20 mins

Servings per Recipe: 4
Calories	534.8
Fat	24.8g
Cholesterol	15.2mg
Sodium	1501.3mg
Carbohydrates	72.7g
Protein	10.9g

Ingredients
2 C. small shell pasta
1 C. mayonnaise
2 C. chunky salsa
1 tbsp chopped fresh cilantro
6 green onions, chopped
1 C. cooked corn
1 C. sliced black olives

1 red pepper, chopped
1/2 tsp onion salt
1/4 tsp cayenne pepper

Directions
1. In a large pan of the lightly salted boiling water, prepare the pasta according to the package's directions.
2. Drain well.
3. In a large bowl add the remaining ingredients and mix till well combined.
4. Add the pasta and toss to coat.
5. Refrigerate to chill before serving.

MAQUE CHOUX
(Native American Style Corn Salad)

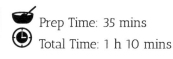

Prep Time: 35 mins
Total Time: 1 h 10 mins

Servings per Recipe: 6
Calories	211 kcal
Fat	11.1 g
Carbohydrates	22.8g
Protein	8.6 g
Cholesterol	14 mg
Sodium	371 mg

Ingredients
6 ears corn, husked and cleaned
2 tablespoons vegetable oil
1 large onion, thinly sliced
1 cup green bell pepper, chopped
1 large fresh tomato, chopped
1/4 cup milk

salt to taste
cayenne pepper
1/4 cup chopped green onions
8 strips crisply cooked turkey bacon, crumbled

Directions
1. Remove the kernels of corn from your ears into a bowl. Slice the ears again to get the milk into the same bowl.
2. Get your oil hot in a frying pan then combine in your green pepper, and onion. Stir fry the mix for 7 mins then combine in the milk, corn, and tomatoes. Stir everything then set the heat to low, and let the mix gently cook for 22 mins while stirring often. But do not let the mix get so hot that begin to boil.
3. Now add some cayenne and salt then set the heat lower and place a lid on the pan. Let everything cook for 7 more minx then add the bacon and green onions.
4. Enjoy.

Ceviche
Guatemala Style

Prep Time: 30 mins
Total Time: 1 day 30 mins

Servings per Recipe: 4
Calories   238.1
Fat   2.8g
Cholesterol   286.4mg
Sodium   1648.7mg
Carbohydrates   20.0g
Protein   33.5g

Ingredients

4 large tomatoes, diced
2 lbs medium shrimp, peeled and deveined
1 onion, diced
1 bunch cilantro, diced
1 jalapeno, diced
12 lemons, squeezed
8 tbsp ketchup

2 tsp Worcestershire sauce
salt and pepper

Directions

1. In a pan of boiling water, blanch the shrimp for about 5 minutes.
2. Transfer into the bowl of ice cold water.
3. Strain when cooled.
4. Transfer the shrimps into the bowl.
5. Add lemon juice and refrigerate to marinate for about 2 hours.
6. Add salt, pepper, ketchup, Worcestershire sauce, onion, tomatoes, chilies and cilantro and refrigerate to marinate for about 2 hours.
7. Serve with some nice crackers.

CHIPOTLE
Cannellini Burgers

🍳 Prep Time: 30 mins
🕐 Total Time: 45 mins

Servings per Recipe: 5
Calories	427.6
Fat	18.5g
Cholesterol	255.0mg
Sodium	1761.7mg
Carbohydrates	48.8g
Protein	116.2g

Ingredients
2 C. cooked red quinoa
1 C. cannellini beans, mashed
1/2 C. panko breadcrumbs
1 large egg, lightly beaten
1 garlic clove, grated
1 tsp dried chipotle powder
1/2 tsp salt
1/2 tsp pepper

3/4 C. sharp cheddar cheese, shredded
3 tbsps olive oil
4 your favorite hamburger buns

Directions
1. Get a mixing bowl: Add the quinoa, mashed cannellini beans, bread crumbs, egg, garlic, chipotle chili powder, salt and pepper. Combine them well. Add the cheese and combine them well.

2. Shape the mix into 5 cakes and refrigerate it for 5 min.

3. Place a large skillet on medium heat. Heat 1 tbsp of oil in it. Add the cakes and cook them for 6 min on each side. Place a slice of cheese of cheese on each cake.

4. Put on the lid and cook them for 2 min until the cheese melts. Assemble your burgers with your favorite toppings. Serve them right away.

5. Enjoy.

Beast
Burger

🥣 Prep Time: 15 mins
🕐 Total Time: 25 mins

Servings per Recipe: 10
Calories	437 kcal
Fat	27.7 g
Carbohydrates	9 g
Protein	36.1 g
Cholesterol	158 mg
Sodium	5863 mg

Ingredients

3 lbs lean ground beef
1/2 medium potato, shredded
1 tbsp minced garlic
12 oz. crumbled blue cheese
2 tsps seasoned salt, or to taste
Freshly ground black pepper to taste
1/2 medium onion, chopped

1/4 C. Worcestershire sauce
2 eggs, beaten
1/2 C. dry bread crumbs

Directions

1. Before you do anything preheat the oven to 350 F.
2. Get a large mixing bowl: Add all the ingredients and mix them well. Shape the mix into 10 thick burger cakes. Cook them in the grill for 6 min on each side.
3. Assemble your burgers with your favorite toppings. Serve them right away.
4. Enjoy.

PARMESAN
Kernels Burger

Prep Time: 45 mins
Total Time: 50 mins

Servings per Recipe: 4
Calories   313.3
Fat   18.5g
Cholesterol   252.0mg
Sodium   1338.7mg
Carbohydrates   27.1g
Protein   11.2g

Ingredients
2 ounces olive oil
3 tbsps diced red onions
2 tbsps diced black olives
2 tbsps diced red bell peppers
1/2 potato, boiled
3 tbsps sweet whole kernel corn
1 tsp diced jalapeno
1 1/2 tbsps diced garlic
4 ounces black beans, drained
4 ounces kidney beans, drained
4 ounces white beans, drained
1/2 tsp chili powder

1 tsp dried oregano
1 tbsp minced fresh parsley leaves
1 tsp red chili pepper flakes
1/2 tsp ground cumin
1 tsp celery salt
1/4 tsp ground sage
2 tbsps seasoned bread crumbs
1/4 C. grated parmesan cheese
1 egg

Directions
1. Bring a salted pot of water to a boil. Add the potato and cook it until it becomes soft. Place it aside to lose heat.

2. Place a large skillet. Add 1 ounce of oil and cook in it the onion with bell peppers and jalapeno. Cook them for 5 min. Place the mix aside to lose heat.

3. Stir in half of the cooked potato with black, kidney and white beans. Mix them well. Stir in the remaining ingredients. Mix them well. Shape the mix into 4 burgers. Place them in the fridge for 5 min.

4. Place a large skillet on medium heat. Add the burgers and cook them for 4 min on each side. Assemble your burgers with your favorite toppings. Serve them right away.

5. Enjoy.

Cheesy
Italian Pizza Burger

Prep Time: 15 mins
Total Time: 30 mins

Servings per Recipe: 16
Calories	322 kcal
Fat	19.1 g
Carbohydrates	18.6g
Protein	18.9 g
Cholesterol	66 mg
Sodium	953 mg

Ingredients

2 lbs ground beef
1 (12 oz.) container fully cooked luncheon meat (e.g. Spam), cubed, optional
12 oz. processed cheese food, cubed
2 small onions, chopped
1 (10.75 oz.) can condensed tomato soup
1 (6 oz.) can tomato paste

1/2 tsp garlic salt
1 1/2 tsps dried oregano
8 hamburger buns split

Directions

1. Before you do anything preheat the oven to 350 F.
2. Place a large skillet on medium heat. Add the beef and cook it for 12 min. discard the fat.
3. Get a food processor: Add the luncheon meat, cheese and onion combine them until they become chopped.
4. Get a mixing bowl: Add the chopped onion mix with beef, tomato soup, tomato paste, garlic salt, and oregano. Mix them well.
5. Spoon the beef mix into the burger buns. Place them on a lined up baking sheet. Cook them in the oven for 1 min. Serve your burgers warm right away.
6. Enjoy.

Made in the USA
Las Vegas, NV
02 June 2021

24053127R00059